# THE

# STANDARD

# BEARER

## WISDOM FROM AMERICA'S

## HEARTLAND

## REGINA SHANK

Spring Mill Publishing

Sharpsburg, Maryland USA

First Printing: 2016

ISBN: 978-0-9835857-4-9

Cover design by Amani Hanson (Becoming Studios).

Editing, text design and typesetting by Jim Bryson (JamesLBryson@gmail.com).

Proofreading by Emilyanne Zornes (pcome.proofandcopy@ gmail.com) .

# Endorsements

Regina Shank is a leader who represents the style of new-model leadership emerging on the scene today. She has painted a clear picture with her words on the pages of this book. As they are applied, the significant nuggets of wisdom found herein will bring about a more excellent way of life. Regina is a state leader, a prophetic voice, a teacher of present day truth, but most of all, an enduring friend. Susan and I are privileged to walk out an endearing friendship with her. As you read these pages, expect to be challenged, encouraged and changed.

May God's richest blessing be upon Regina, and all who read this book.

Clay Nash

Author of <u>Relational Authority</u> and <u>Activating the Prophetic</u>

Apostolic Leader of *The CityGate*, Southhaven, MS and Network Ekklesia International

*****

I am enjoying the book God has placed on Regina's heart. I consider her thoughts on paper to be bits of wisdom gained through the experience of observing and working with all kinds of people over the years. I really like the title and chapters, which go beyond the religious "how to" books on the market today. It gives clarity to a life lived normally, yet wrapped with truths from the Word of God. A blessed book for our generation.

Apostle Raymond Mabion

*Kansas City Prayer Dome*

Bethlehem Christian Assembly

I have known and worked with Regina Shank for well over 15 years. She loves the Lord and is dedicated to helping people receive the freedom that only Christ Jesus provides. Regina also desires to see the nations transformed to look more like the Kingdom of Heaven than the domain of darkness. Her prophetic insight will help us to further our walk with the Lord and be the salt and light we are called to be.

Joe Nicola

Pastor – New Covenant Ministries

Author of <u>Ekklesia– The Government of the Kingdom of Heaven on Earth</u>

*****

Regina Shank knows the power of prayer and the power of turning your life fully over to the Lord. In her book, <u>The Standard Bearer</u>, she reveals truth based on the Word of God, sealed by her own personal experience of allowing the liberty of God's Word to become reality in daily life. This book is a catalyst that will ignite the cleansing fire of His Spirit within you.

Lisa Bickle Stribling

Director, *Hope City*, IHOP K.C.

Author – <u>One Last Vein</u>

# Dedication

This book is dedicated to all who are seeking freedom, abundant life and fulfillment of the unrequited dreams in their hearts. Because I have been one who has experienced the need for Divine intervention in order to come into what has been promised, I release to you in this book a portion of what I have learned. The pain of despair, the loss of direction, the devastation of hope deferred hits the human heart causing it to wonder and wander. Finding your path to Life is easier if someone points you in the right direction. Perhaps my shared life experiences, with the revelatory input based on the Word of God, will be markers on your journey to point you to Life Himself. There is a standard to follow that will lead us to victory. I dedicate this book to you and the multitudes of others who have been through the wilderness and have found the substance of faith. Song of Solomon 3:6 says,

> *Who is this coming up from the wilderness like a column of smoke, perfumed with myrrh and incense made from all the spices of the merchant?*

May your heart be revived!

# Contents

# Contents (continued)

# Contents (continued)

# Foreword

Wisdom is essential to success in life. People with wisdom are those who know secrets leading to breakthrough and goals attained. Those without wisdom usually end up frustrated and living a life of hope deferred. The Bible says this causes their hearts to be sick, no longer able to dream and believe (Proverbs 13:12). When this occurs, real life is over and existence-only has begun. Wisdom that brings success is critical to a healthy spiritual heart. The scripture says that God's wisdom cries out in the streets.

> *Wisdom calls aloud outside; she raises her voice in the open squares.*

> Proverbs 1:20 NKJV

This means that wisdom is all around us if we will just open our eyes and ears to recognize it. It is accessible to all who have a heart for it. In The Standard Bearer, we are given nuggets of wisdom. This wisdom, valued and applied, can alter our life for the good. It can move us from "just doing life" to "living the dream" God has placed in our hearts.

It is God's heart for us to live life with passion. As we take to ourselves the wisdom of God and let it adjust our lives, our hearts can come alive again. The heart which was dead and lifeless will spring to life. The God we serve is a God of resurrection. This is what Jesus said. His words are spirit and they are life (John 6:63).

I challenge you to let the words of wisdom in this book bring life to any dead place in you. The Spirit of the living Christ will move through these words and bring life to your soul! When this happens, everything changes!

Blessings,

Robert Henderson

Robert Henderson Ministries

# Introduction

Processing life, and finding purpose in it, is a lifelong endeavor. Finding your place in the sun, putting up your umbrella, and staking your claim to life's adventures establishes you in time. Your place in the sun is usually determined by your parents. Your umbrella represents your protection from harmful influences. And staking your claim gives you a starting place from which to explore and experience life. Yet many people do not find their place in the sun; and if they do, their understanding of personal purpose is yet to be discovered. Those who have wonderful parents receive a protective umbrella and, from that position, have a foothold from which to stake their claim on an abundant life. But that claim is not valid without facing the claim holder—the One who redeemed us from sin and self-destruction. Jesus said, "The thief comes only to steal and kill and destroy; I came that they may have life, and have it abundantly"(John 10:10).

Finding abundant life starts with Life Himself—Jesus Christ. He put you here for a purpose and determined the time and place you were to live. Acts 17:26-28 says,

> *From one man he made all the nations, that they should inhabit the whole earth; and he marked out their appointed times in history and the boundaries of their lands. God did this so that they would seek him and perhaps reach out for him and find him, though he is not far from any one of us. "For in him*

*we live and move and have our being." As some of*
*your own poets have said, "We are his offspring."*

For those who were born into abusive situations or dysfunctional families, the path is the same, although they must reclaim their stake, as it is possibly being occupied by usurpers.

In my work with the poor and my relationships with the affluent, I hear the same cry for help coming from the core of their beings. Navigation of life demands a relationship with the Navigator. He both placed us here and wrote the plan for our lives before we were born. Psalm 139:16 says,

> *Your eyes have seen my unformed substance, and in your book were all written the days that were ordained for me, when as yet there was not one of them.*

Rather than write our own Book of Life, we are invited to step into His plan released to us before we were substance. Because of our independent attitudes, our soul's lust of the flesh, and the pride of life, we can wander through life from pleasure to pleasure, or from disaster to disaster, never realizing we were not meant to steer our own lives without direction and input from Wisdom Himself. Many times, I have reached out for wisdom and guidance from the Lord and found Him ready to answer my cry for help and direction in life.

Many analogies have been written describing the Divine intervention of the Creator on our behalf. He is the footprints in the sand, the lighthouse on the shore, the lifeboat sent to our sinking ship, the shepherd searching for His lost sheep, the door of hope in hopeless situations, the stag on the mountain, the Savior on a cross, the wind and the fire, the Resurrection and the Life. But He is also the still small voice longing to lead us with wisdom we do not have. Ecclesiastes says,

*Wisdom is better than weapons of war, but one sinner destroys much good.*

Ecclesiastes 9:18

Some of the battles we are now desiring to win could possibly have been avoided by the voice of wisdom.

In writing this book, I have chosen morsels of wisdom from many sources: the Word of God, personal experiences, relationships, and difficult encounters with life's problems. I have experienced the truth that the Lord makes a way where there is no way. He is the door of hope in the Valley of Achor, the valley of trouble. (See Hosea 2:15)

I wrote these articles with you in mind, to help on your journey through life. May these morsels of wisdom help you avoid the pitfalls and entrapments of the enemy. May you find your place in the earth and leave a big footprint of Godly influence to those who would come after. Without the foundation of the Truth of the Word of God, we can be tossed around by opinions and agendas of man. In this book, my desire is to lift up the Banner of Truth for all to see and follow.

Isaiah 59:14 (AMP) says,

*Justice is turned away backward, and righteousness (uprightness and right standing with God) stands far off; for truth has fallen in the street (the city's forum), and uprightness cannot enter (the courts of justice).*

It's time for the banner of Truth to be raised up again. Truth is a person. Jesus tells us: "I Am the Way, and the Truth, and the Life (John 14:6).

# I

# FREEDOM

*Lord,*

*I know that freedom is internal as well as external. You said that you came to set the captives free. Free us from the bondages of fear, intimidation, offense, pride, and rebellion. Open our hearts to the input of your Spirit. You have spoken to us in your Word that where the Spirit of the Lord is, there is freedom, emancipation from bondage. Free our hearts to know you; free our minds to think your thoughts; free our bodies from the bondages of sin; and free a generation from cultural influences that tend to nullify and water down the power of your Word. Your Word stands forever! Help me stand on the strong foundation of Truth that is portrayed through your Son Jesus Christ and demonstrated in the Word of Truth. Amen*

# Truth Or Fiction

Belief systems are interesting because we believe them.

For instance, consider the historic belief that the earth is flat. People believed that if you sailed far enough, you would fall off the earth and into an abyss. This belief held mankind in fear and close to land for centuries, limiting exploration and discovery.

Another example is the belief in the medical benefits of blood-letting. When a person was sick, the physician would cut a vein to allow the "bad blood" to drain out, thus making the patient well. Turns out, the issue was not with bad blood; it was with an incorrect perception causing life—good blood—to be drained from an ailing body. At that point, the sickness became a minor issue compared to death by anemia.

Fortunately, we now know that these archaic perceptions were gross errors. But have you ever examined your own belief systems for accuracy? Perhaps we too operate on a faulty system of erroneous concepts based on nothing but hearsay, tradition, or narrow experience. Knowing the truth will set you free from error—even save your life.

So how do we know what we believe is accurate? What standard do we use to discover the errors in our own thinking?

Truth is not a concept, precept, or supposition. Truth is not what we believe, but *Who* we believe. Truth is a person. Jesus said in John

14:6, "I am the Way, the Truth, and the Life." So our basis for truth comes from the Word of God through the manifested representation of that Word of Truth, Who is Jesus, as explained to me through Holy Spirit who is called the "Spirit of Truth."

> *But when He, the Spirit of truth, comes, He will guide you into all the truth; for He will not speak on His own initiative, but whatever He hears, He will speak; and He will disclose to you what is to come.*

John 16:13(NASB)

As a person who can be deceived, I can choose to be a seeker of Truth—one who desires a foundation for life, a solid place to stand, not tossed back and forth by politicians, persuaders, or pied-pipers seeking a following. By pursuing a relationship with the Spirit of Truth and standing on the solid foundation of the Word of God, we can grow in the knowledge of Truth and free ourselves from the gross errors in thinking that pervade the blood-letting culture of today.

Are you ready to take the challenge? Here it is: ask the Spirit of Truth to show you where your thinking patterns are more in line with world culture than the Word of Truth that is the foundation for abundant life. May we "seek" and find what all of us are looking for, freedom to live in Truth and knowledge from the One who knows all.

# The Creeping Critter

*For the Spirit God gave us does not make us timid,*
*but gives us power, love and self-discipline.*

II Timothy 1:7

Insects are such a nuisance! I've decided their only purpose is to keep pesticide companies in business. Personally, I love to sit on my back deck and enjoy nice weather. The problem comes when the insects enjoy it with me. They buzz around my head, waiting for the right moment to strike. When they do, the welt rises, the itch starts, and the loss of a few blood cells is a reality. We fight back with a bug zapper, a can of pesticide spray, and a few citronella candles, but a few always slip past our defenses.

Fear is a lot like those insects. It buzzes around in your head, tormenting you with dread, while you wonder when its sting will strike. There are people who live their lives looking at life through fear spectacles. That perspective can come through past traumas, through words spoken to us by abusive authorities, or through fear-based people who have influenced us. The problem with fear is that it can paralyze our lives and keep us caged up in worry, anxiety, and dread.

Escaping the safety of the cage is difficult because fear warns us to not venture beyond our narrow controlled environment. Fear has a friend called *Control,* that tries to keep everything in order so there are no surprises. The problem escalates when the buzz in your head comes in for a strike.

On our front porch, we discovered a wasp nest in our light fixture. Inside the nest were small larvae destined to become wasps. We destroyed the larvae, took down the nest and cleaned up our porch. In the same way, fear thoughts have to be discovered and destroyed before they become dangerous to our freedom and abundant life. The Bible says it this way,

> *We demolish arguments and every pretension that sets itself up against the knowledge of God, and we take captive every thought to make it obedient to Christ.*

> II Corinthians 10:5

We destroy the larvae before it becomes an aggressive pest, not only in setting up a nest on the porch but also by propagating the sting of fear in our hearts and minds.

According to Psychology Today:

> *Chronic stress and elevated cortisol levels also increase risk for depression, mental illness, and lower life expectancy.... Cortisol is released in response to fear or stress by the adrenal glands as part of the fight-or-flight mechanism.*

No wonder the Bible says 365 times to *Fear Not!* That's one for every day of the year.

So how do we get rid of fear?

First, we recognize the negative thought, then we replace it with a positive one. Find those 365 scriptures that say *Fear Not!* and read them every time those thoughts come.

Second, we must know the truth. Michel de Montaigne said: *My life has been filled with terrible misfortune; most of which never happened.* According to one study, at least 85% of what we worry about never happens.

Third, we surround ourselves with positive people. Personally, I would rather be with a Tigger than an Eeyore. (From The Adventures of Winnie the Pooh.)

Fourth, remember the promise in Jeremiah 29:11,

> *"For I know the plans I have for you," declares the Lord. "Plans to prosper you and not to harm you, plans to give you hope and a future."*

Trust the Lord. Take those negative thoughts captive, destroy the larvae, read those *Fear Not!* scriptures, and choose your friends wisely.

Abundant life awaits you!

# My Lot In Life

It's just my lot in life.

This common phrase expresses people's feeling that circumstances are beyond their control. And while I can sympathize with them, listening closer reveals how they have settled for less than an abundant life. There can even be a tinge of regret for the choices that brought them to this place of resignation. But behind that tinge lurks the real culprit—the blame and anger leading to depression, and the resultant loss of dreams. That's the worst part of this scenario!

Someone was in my office last week and we talked about the word "lot". The Hebrew root is *goral*, meaning "a pebble." That same word is in Psalm 16:5 denoting "a portion" or "an inheritance or destiny as assigned by God."

It can also mean, "that by which the fate or portion of one is determined; that by which an event is committed to chance, that is, to the determination of providence; as, to cast lots; to draw lots."

Yet these definitions are a bit contradictory to one another, aren't they? One says our lot is determined by fate, and the other says it is by providence. Fate and providence are totally different entities. Let's look at Psalm 16:5 for further insight.

> *Lord, you alone are my portion and my cup; you make my lot secure.*

Perhaps the confusion between fate and providence comes from the biblical practice of casting lots. It was like drawing straws or rolling dice, except they used pebbles. They would "draw lots," believing this would determine the will of the Lord in a situation. With the Lord overseeing this practice, the lot was chosen by Him. But if it was done without His intervention, the lot could be determined by fate. So the lot in life took on the idea that some unknown force could bring forth an existence not of our choosing or because of our wrong choosing.

This bears the mark of victimhood. When we believe some unknown force rules over our lives and brought us to this lot, the delusion in our thinking seals our "fate." It's as if our personal choice of accepting our lot is the true power of fate.

I personally don't believe in fate, nor do I believe we are stuck in a place called my lot in life. Psalm 16:5 shows us the Lord can make our lot secure. When He enters, the whole lot changes. Actually, a whole lot changes. What appears to be a place of entrapment transforms into a place of freedom with the arrival of the Spirit of the Lord.

> *Now the Lord is the Spirit, and where the Spirit of the Lord is, there is freedom.*

> II Corinthians 3:17

Let us invite the Lord into our lot, whether it was determined by a roll of the dice or the Lord Himself, and see what He will do with it. Every good and perfect gift comes from Him, so abundant life can come to any situation or lot we find ourselves in. Rather than relegating our lives to what is handed to us, let us take the reins and turn our lives toward the truth.

A life turned over to the Lord gains an inheritance beyond our fondest expectations.

# Breaking Free

*He lifted me out of the slimy pit, out of the mud and mire; he set my feet on a rock and gave me a firm place to stand. He put a new song in my mouth, a hymn of praise to our God. Many will see and fear the Lord and put their trust in him.*

Psalm 40:2-3

Many people choose to give in to hopelessness and victimhood, believing they are powerless over their circumstances. These people fall prey to whatever trouble life throws at them, but it doesn't have to be this way. Letting go of past traumas, conflicts, and loss brings tremendous change and transformation. The power to live an abundant life has been given to all of us, but we must reach out and take it.

Change starts on the inside as we humble ourselves and seek our Creator who loves us and leads us into all truth (John 8:32).

I wrote this poem while meditating on the choices we have as creatures of the world seeking to rise above its grip.

# Don't Shut Down

*Selfish shutdown comes around*
*When feelings press to overwhelm.*
*Taken to the underground*
*Revolving 'round a clanging sound.*
*The gong of fear, the peal of pride*
*Choosing to remain inside.*
*It digs its path through darkened cave*
*Owning the heart, making a slave.*

*Left to hide in darkness' den*
*It speaks of hope that might have been.*
*It tells its tale again and again*
*Rehearsing with anger to its self-sorry friend.*
*The familiar story goes like this*
*As it whispers in the darkness.*
*You have a right to bitter stance*
*Tripping and falling at every chance.*

*Blame and Shame follow Pride*
*Encamped upon the hillside.*
*Homeless first, they find the way*
*To enter in the victim's cave.*
*They stir the flames of latent ire,*
*Warm themselves and feed the fire.*
*What grows within, birthed by pride,*
*Will grow so big it cannot hide.*

*To cut its roots, abort its schemes,*
*Requires humility at the scene.*
*Humble arrives with mirror in hand,*
*Turning the head of prideful man.*

Seeing himself mirrored in pain,
Losing reality's truthful refrain,
Prideful man drops his bluff,
Stomps his foot, he's had enough.

The darkened cave fills with light,
Blame and Shame flee with fright.
Bursting forth from sweet surrender,
The fount of joy spews its render.
Finally freed from sticky slime,
The man stands free, no longer blind.
And speaks forth with his new-found breath
Words of utter faithfulness:

It's not an inward self-sorry life,
But letting go of bitter strife
That raises hearts from Hope deferred
To living life—others preferred.

# Fumbled, Foiled, Or Fused

I'm not a football fan but my husband is, so I am exposed to some of the colorful terms. One of my favorites is *fumbled*. Evidently, if the ball is dropped while in play, it is fumbled. I like the word. It has a certain lilt to it. That rhythmic swing doesn't describe its impact, though, and even in describing the word, I have fumbled.

Another word, historically used by black-cloaked villains in the classic "damsel in distress" movies, is *foiled*. Ask the younger generation to define *foiled* and you will probably hear about aluminum foil. In truth, when the movie villain was outwitted, he would exclaim in frustration: *Curses! Foiled again!* No, he wasn't wrapped in aluminum; he was foiled, meaning he was *prevented from succeeding*.

Fused is another interesting word, in that it does not come from the word confused. Although this can be confusing, fused actually means to join or combine into one unit—unless you are talking about defusing dynamite that is about to blow.

So, have you fumbled your opportunities, been foiled in your goals, or been fused together with the world? The good news is this: there is hope for all of us fumbled, foiled, and fused people.

You can pick up that fumbled goal that you dropped previously and carry it to the end zone. You might have to change your approach to life, leaving your villain cloak behind, but "foiled again" attitudes can be replaced with success as you decide to escape the railroad tracks of the failure train. Finding that new road to fulfillment takes some seeking, but it can be found with the help of the Lord.

Being fused with the world—becoming one with it—presents a bigger problem. Don't forget that we are in the world but not of it.

> *"I have given them your word and the world has hated them, for they are not of the world any more than I am of the world. My prayer is not that you take them out of the world but that you protect them from the evil one. They are not of the world, even as I am not of it."*

> John 17:14-16

Although we walk in the world, we internally separate ourselves from the world's values, attitudes, and perceptions. Instead, we carry within us the hidden treasure of Kingdom life found in relationship with Jesus, looking for opportunity to share Words of life. So become un-fused with the world. Become one with the Lord and leave the con-fuse-ion behind.

Fumbled, foiled, or fused fail flagrantly in their foul feats to foil your future.

# What Do You Think?

As a young person, I loved to be asked, "What do you think?" because it meant someone wanted my opinion. Today I am rarely flattered. I know the question is likely a ploy for the questioner to tell me what he or she thinks. The moment I collect my thoughts for a qualified answer, their interruption will begin.

Clearly, most of us prefer the sound of our own voice over another's, but what does this show us about human nature? (You realize this question is a ploy to tell you what I think, right?) It shows that we value our opinions above the opinions of others… chiefly because they are ours.

Which explains why, when our cherished opinions are found to be wrong, we find ways to backtrack. Let's face it—we want to be right! And although proving a point or seeking personal vindication rarely impresses others, it's the first thing to surface when we find ourselves challenged.

Critical people are especially prone to this tendency. They stand by waiting for a chance to voice opinions that are often stilted, skewed, or ignoble. Not surprisingly, most critics do not like to be challenged, for it could prove them wrong. Consequently, they do not want your response—it threatens their vindication.

> *Vindication is a sweet thing—when you get vindication, you've been proven right or justified in doing something.*

(www.vocabulary.com/dictionary/vindication)

As sweet as vindication feels, however, it can sour relationships. While proving yourself to be right is vital in a court of law, in friendships, it tends to diminish your fan base. So what can we do about this, especially when vindication is not an option?

Here's what I recommend. It goes like this:

*I am wrong!*

Just try saying it. Go on.

*I am w-r-o-n-g!* (Whew!)

I know it can be difficult to let those words out. They stick in the throat and make that choking sound you get with allergic reactions. Not only do they choke off your breath but your humility as well. Best to let them out.

Sometimes when we can't deal directly with an issue, we jokingly say the things that are really on our minds. I recall a vigorous discussion with an acquaintance who, at one point, teasingly said, *"Ah, just put a lid on it!"* It was a joke, I think. Or was it?

Here's my point. Don't get stuck in your own opinions. Don't backdoor your perspective with a joke—that's the cowardly way of stating your point. Cough up your pride and admit you might be wrong.

Being teachable is the first step to wisdom.

> *Wisdom is better than weapons of war.*
>
> Ecclesiastes 9:18

> *But the advantage of knowledge is that wisdom preserves those who have it.*
>
> Ecclesiastes 7:12b

# The Tea Kettle Is Boiling

Frustration is a dangerous thing! It's been around forever. Imagine Eve tasting the forbidden fruit and realizing it wasn't as good as it looked. Imagine Daniel Boone opening a beaver trap and the half-dead beaver bites the hand that trapped it. Imagine Abraham Lincoln studying by firelight when suddenly the fire goes out. Imagine Wilbur and Orville Wright trying to invent the flying machine, but instead of being Wright, they were Wrong… again and again. Imagine...

Well, you get the picture!

We never imagine any of these famous people getting frustrated, but the reality is, they did. It's a human trait, one I don't like and didn't bargain for, but we all have to deal with it, sometimes daily. Things just don't go as planned. The cogs get stuck and the wheel stops. Frustration gives birth to anger; anger starts to boil; blood pressure goes up and productivity goes down. When frustration peaks, the steam has to vent somewhere. Internally, it damages your health; externally it harms your relationships.

I can see Eve hurling the half-fruit at the serpent out of frustration over her huge loss. I can imagine Daniel Boone tossing out a few expletives at beaver daddy. It's hard to picture Abraham Lincoln yelling at his mother or stomping his foot on his school book, but I'm sure he did something non-presidential when the light went out. Orville and Wilbur were brothers, you know. Maybe there were fisticuffs when things didn't go as planned. It's certainly not written in the history books which glamorize our historical figures. But all of us are human and we have to deal with unplanned, frustrating situations.

Reacting to frustration is easier than choosing to walk away from it. The healthy response is to step back a few paces, focus on something else, and analyze your frustrating situation from afar. Find a place away from others to let out that steam. A good healthy *ARGGGHH!* coming from the pit of your stomach never hurt anybody.

Find someone who can help you with the problem. Pulling yourself up by your own bootstraps causes lots of chaffing, and what do you do when the bootstrap breaks?

Finally, don't give up or give in. We are flying today because Orville and Wilbur overcame their frustration without destroying their dream.

Take the kettle off the burner and enjoy your day!

> *"In your anger do not sin": Do not let the sun go down while you are still angry...*

Ephesians 4:26

# Soar Like An Eagle

I felt trapped in my circumstances, feeling there was no way out and that the present situation was entirely my fault because of wrong choices I had made. (Yes, I write long sentences. Hopefully, you get the picture.) The key word here is feeling. Feelings are real, valid, and can be very strong, carrying us to the heights of ecstasy or the verge of suicide and destruction. Feelings come from the soul at the core of our being—the control center for direction, vision, and purpose.

The problem with the soul is that without Christ, it is unredeemed—left to flounder on its own without input and direction from the Source of Life. We were not created to function on our own without direction from our Creator. Until we come to that realization and allow Him to redeem us, we are puppets to our wrong choices, fickle emotions, and analytical brains.

Even after we are redeemed, being led by the soul is still a habit not easily broken without intervention by the Spirit of God. The Bible tells us,

> *For those who are led by the Spirit of God are the children of God.*

> Romans 8:14

Now, if being led by the Spirit is the test of being a child of God, how many of us are passing that test? Another way to put it is this:

Are you a puppet of your feelings, or a child of God? (Aren't you glad I'm not preaching at your church this Sunday?)

Certainly, everybody has negative emotions sometimes, but what do we do with the strong feelings of entrapment, depression, guilt or suicide? First of all, in order to get some light in the room of the soul, you have to turn the light on. That light is Jesus.

> *When Jesus spoke again to the people, he said, "I am the light of the world. Whoever follows me will never walk in darkness, but will have the light of life."*

> John 8:12

At one of our Sunday evening gatherings, I spoke to a man about getting light into his soul. He just wasn't getting it. So I went over to the wall, turned off the lights, and we stood in darkness. The man wasn't familiar with the room exits, so without light, he was stuck unless he felt his way out of the room. When I turned the lights back on, he could see. I explained to him that the soul is like a dark room; it contains all the negatives we have experienced, all the unprocessed feelings, and all the guilt, shame, and blame that come through living in a fallen world. The good news is that with the light of the world shining in our darkness, the relearning process can begin.

Likewise, my feelings of entrapment mentioned earlier were invalidated when the light of the world showed up to "shed light on the subject." In that moment, Jesus spoke something to me I will never forget.

> *"Regina, you need to look up. You are looking at your circumstances instead of seeing from my perspective. There is no lid on your life and you can go as high in me as you desire."*

My perspective changed in an instant; I realized my soul was vying for control of my destiny. Our will is the pilot of the soul with power over our feelings. I made a choice that day to rise above the maze of feelings. I asked the Lord to teach me how to soar above the circumstances life had thrown my way. That day, I began to catch the wind and soar above the storm.

> *But those who hope in the Lord will renew their strength. They will soar on wings like eagles...*

Isaiah 40:31

# II

# IDENTITY

*Father God,*

*Because we are made in your image, help us put down other images that desire to mark us with their identity. We want to look like you, speak like you, and demonstrate your character in the earth. Jesus said in John 14:9, "Anyone who has seen me has seen the Father." May we show forth your image in the earth demonstrating the fruit of knowing you. As your sons and daughters, placed on this earth to bring heaven's will into our sphere of influence, may we step into our identity, quickly walking in the freedom you purchased for us. As we find our identity in you, we are free to be. Keep us from the trap of earning a place when you have already given us favor, forgiveness, and status through the restorative work of Jesus Christ on the cross.*

*In His Name. Amen*

# Beauty Fades... Or Does It?

I always thought others would grow older but not me! I suppose that is a bit arrogant. When the realization hits that time does not stop for ourselves or anyone else, there is a rude awakening. It hit me the other day when I looked in the mirror and saw my mother staring back at me. I've decided that wrinkle cream doesn't work, and cosmetic surgery isn't the best option either. Have you seen Hollywood's version of eternal youth? Let me tell you—skin stretched that far causes the lips to grin like the Cheshire Cat.

So what do you do when youth fades, cellulite encroaches, and the former beach body has its own inner tube?

Fight it tooth and nail!! I've always said: *If the barn needs painting, then paint it!* But even that solution, at best, only masks the problem. Putting on all that paint in the morning and stripping it off each night can't be good for the bank account or the weathered skin.

Beauty is promised, produced, and packaged for purchase online, at the mall, and on the home shopping network. I know. I've tried it all: beauty jar, beauty bar, beauty line, beauty time, beauty soap, beauty swill, beauty bath, beauty pill. And still, all I see is my mother with a shiny face staring back at me.

So if you can't buy beauty and you can't stop time, what options do you have? The Bible tells us,

*Your beauty should not come from outward adornment, such as elaborate hairstyles and the wearing of gold jewelry or fine clothes. Rather, it should be that of your inner self, the unfading beauty of a gentle and quiet spirit, which is of great worth in God's sight.*

I Peter 3:3-4

Outward adornment isn't bad, but true beauty comes from within. It's inward, not outward.

Since I can't buy unfading beauty in a jar, I choose to focus on developing the inner beauty of the gentle and quiet spirit. And perhaps when we observe others, we could look beyond the surface for a heart that has grown beautiful over the years. Inner beauty does not fade with time but shines through both youth and old age.

*He has made everything beautiful in its time. He has also set eternity in the human heart...*

Ecclesiastes 3: 11

Beauty from the heart takes time to grow. This is the hope of the children of God who live in eternity. Only the outward shell fades. I remember my grandmother at age 90 telling me she felt 30 years old inside. What a precious legacy! I've decided age is not a number but a state of mind. It's okay to grow old outside—indeed, it is inevitable—but I choose to never grow old inside.

Let the eternal beauty of a gentle and quiet spirit shine from your heart.

# Stolen Identity

H as your identity been stolen?

I remember the day we received a letter from the IRS. It was addressed to me and an unknown man. After assuring my husband that he had not been replaced, we opened the letter and realized someone had filed my taxes using my social security number and sent papers to the IRS to get my refund. (Oh, the gall of identity thieves!) Fortunately, the IRS thought it was bogus and sent a letter to us for verification. We took it to our accountant who contacted the IRS and stopped the fraud. Since we always file jointly, the scam was easy to spot. Still, many people are not so fortunate and lose thousands of dollars. Identity theft has become so prevalent, there are now companies to protect people from this insidious crime.

All of which got me to thinking…

How do we identify ourselves? Speaking your name is a great way to describe who you are, but you are not the only one with that name. Your social security number helps identify you, but that can be stolen, as my story describes. How about a passport or driver's license? All of these confirm identity, but they are outward identifiers—easily copied, forged or stolen.

True identity must come from within, but who are we on the inside? Our attempts to answer that question tell us much about ourselves. We often identify ourselves by our life history, our occupation, or our income level. In helping the poor of our city, I observe people who label themselves based on their need. More affluent people identify themselves by their social standing, the house they live in, or the jewelry they wear.

I believe identity is an inward picture of who we are. It is influenced by several factors, among them: words spoken by others, life experiences, family upbringing, cultural heritage and spiritual condition. So what you do is not who you are! What you wear is not who you are! What you need is not who you are!

John gives us a true picture of identity.

> *Jesus knew that the Father had put all things under his power, and that he had come from God and was returning to God; so he got up from the meal, took off his outer clothing, and wrapped a towel around his waist. After that, he poured water into a basin and began to wash his disciples' feet, drying them with the towel that was wrapped around him.*

John 13:3-5

Because Jesus had his identity secure—he knew where He came from and where He was going—he could serve others without feeling it was beneath Him. We, too, can know who we are as children of God, knowing we came into this earth for a purpose; knowing who we belong to and where we are going at the end of our sojourn.

So the question remains: *Has your identity been stolen?* If so, you can get it back by receiving the purpose of God for your life. Remember:

You are *not* who you think you are.

You are *not* who people say you are.

You are *not* what you do.

You are created in the image of God to reflect His nature and fulfill the purpose for which you were born. Don't let circumstances or other people label you. Get your identity back. Know who you are. Know where you are going.

Take the towel and serve.

# Song Of Life

*Deadlines and commitments*
*Emails and equipment*
*Flat tires and road rage*
*Toothaches and old age*
*Stress and stomachaches*
*Anxiety and headaches.*

Sound familiar? Sorry Virginia, there is no Santa Claus. And the world Norman Rockwell painted is a fantasy land at best. Yet life goes on.

How do we function in an unpredictable world? Some people swear. Others hit the gym. Many turn to sedatives or antidepressants. A few go fishing…or shopping.

Whatever coping skills we resort to, if we're not careful, we can develop an attitude of victimhood. Just today, a young clerk in a retail store stood on a ladder and claimed that if it was going to fall, it would be when he was on it. Personally, I don't believe in bad luck, nor do I believe the young man had been singled out by some unknown force to fall. (And to prove my point, he stayed upright!)

Dealing with the reality of unexpected trials is part of the journey we call *life*. Yet facing these obstacles head-on can take its toll on our strength. Here's how to walk through stressful places without losing it:

1. Realize the stressful situation is a temporary one. Tomorrow will come and the trial will be a day closer to being over.

2. Stay calm and respond to the situation instead of allowing it to dictate how you feel.

3. Ask for help. Personally, I ask the Lord for wisdom, strength, and His perspective on the situation. I also ask family and friends for counsel and emotional support. We weren't meant to walk through life alone.

4. Recognize that feelings don't have to dictate your actions.

5. Find a time and place to process the difficult situation. Write about it, talk to a friend, or pray about it. Don't internalize the stress lest it cause bitterness in your soul.

*Laugh with a friend*
*Go for a drive*
*Sit by a river*
*Be glad you're alive*
*Dig in the dirt*
*Kick off your shoes*
*Lie in the grass*
*Feel the dew*
*Sing to the Lord*
*At the top of your lungs*
*Give thanks for your life*
*Your joy's just begun.*

Yes, Virginia, even though there is no Santa Claus, there are things to sing about.

We all face unplanned, overwhelming situations. Don't reside in the land of trouble. Make it a temporary drive-through. Never judge tomorrow by the events of yesterday. Let hope lead you to new horizons.

And don't forget to sing! Make a joyful noise!

# The Standard Of Truth

When Adam and Eve tasted of the tree of knowledge of good and evil, they lost connection with the tree of life. Previously, they walked and talked with God. But after their disobedience, everything changed. Our redemption came through the sacrifice of the Son of God at Calvary. This act of purchase made our relationship with God possible again. Yet even in this restoration of relationship, we must choose to tap into the spirit of God within us. We are spirit, have a soul and presently live in a body. "Deep calls to deep" (Psalm 42:7).

Once we tasted of the forbidden fruit, we became dependent on our own senses and reasoning rather than being led by God's Spirit. Romans 8:14 says, "For those who are led by the Spirit of God are the children of God."

We have a choice to not only receive Jesus as our Redeemer but also to be led by the Spirit of God within us. The alternative is to be led by solely our mind and emotions.

So what voice are you listening to?

We can filter our internal thoughts through the foundation of the Word of God. For instance, if we hear an internal voice that moves us toward unbiblical behavior, we know to evaluate our motives. Certainly, we can rationalize all we want, but the Word of God stands forever. Without this firm foundation, we will be tossed to and fro by opinions of man, including those of our own thought life.

We were never meant to be led by our own limited resources. God likes opinionated people—which is fortunate for many of us—but opinion is not a good foundation unless it has been formulated by Truth. Facts are not necessarily truth. The Bible calls Holy Spirit the Spirit of Truth. See John 16. As we read the Word of Truth, empowered by the Spirit of Truth, we are less likely to be misled, confused or deceived.

How would you like to tap into the fountain of all wisdom? We have access to the wisdom of God through our personal relationship with Him restored through Jesus Christ.

I've had this reoccurring dream that we are troops fighting in an ancient battle. Except that the standard bearer, who is supposed to hold the flag before the troops, has been removed. Instead of waving free, the banner lays in the dirt. In my dream, I race to pick it up and raise it high so it can be followed by the warriors.

I believe that in today's culture, the standard of the Truth of God's Word has fallen and we are called to raise it high again. Truth is a person. (John 14:6) Raise Him high.

# Perception or Reality

What we think we know may just be what we think.

Many people have an elevated view of their own negative thoughts, believing them to be reality. Worse, the bad experiences which spawned these thoughts compound that false sense of reality, molding the person's life through successive disappointments, sealing their fate as experience after experience further entraps them—a self-replicating cycle of doom.

Which of course begs the question: What's worse? A cocked-eyed optimist or a self-sorry pessimist?

(Don't answer that question. It's a distraction from the real issue.)

By now you probably think I'm going to equivocate by telling you to be balanced in your thinking. Actually, it's a bit stronger than that. Here is where we are going: Some thoughts will kill you! That's right—dead. They do it all the time. "For the wages of sin is death" (Romans 6:23).

Killer thoughts deliver condemnation, shame, blame, fear, guilt, even self-loathing and self-punishment. Regret soon follows, opening the door to depression which is really oppression in disguise. These thoughts kill dreams, hope, and confidence, damaging forward progress. Vision for the future is destroyed by evidence from the past. The end result is a victim mentality, opening the door to a fresh round of death-wielding experiences and conclusions.

What a predicament! To be sealed in a plastic container of negativity, held captive by life's bad experiences rather than life-giving reality. This reeks of bondage; a morbid matrix of our own making.

But there is a way out. Kill the killer thoughts! The Bible says to take them captive.

> *We demolish arguments and every pretension that sets itself up against the knowledge of God, and we take captive every thought to make it obedient to Christ.*

(2 Corinthians 10:5)

It's simple. If we don't capture them, they will capture us.

I remember talking with a woman who wanted a divorce. She told me all the things her husband was doing wrong. The list was long and her heart was heavy. I waited for her to take a breath. She finally looked at me and declared that she had married the wrong person. (Oh how Hollywood has skewed our thinking!) I asked her to take a notebook and list two things he did that were right. Her mind was so full of his faults that it took a while to shift her thinking. She eventually wrote that he went to work every day and was good to the children.

My counsel to her was to thank God for these two attributes every day for a week, asking Him to show her more. After prayer for her heart to change, she went home to do her assignment. Fortunately, she continued to shift her thinking until her heart changed. She realized that false expectations sowed into her from unrealistic "Happily Ever After" movies had filled her mind with delusions about love. Today her marriage is well and growing.

So, perception is not necessarily reality; perceptions can be changed. Proverbs says, "For as he <a man> thinks within himself, so he is" (Proverbs 23:7).

As the heart changes, so does the man. The Word also says in Proverbs,

> *In the Lord's hand the king's heart is a stream of water that he channels toward all who please him.*

> Proverbs 21:1

The key is to yield the heart to the One who can turn it toward truth, bringing freedom. We can have the mind of Christ. (I Corinthians 2:16)

# III

# OPPORTUNITY

*Lord,*

*I Corinthians 16:9 speaks of a wide door of opportunity for effectual service has been opened to us. Help us to recognize that door and walk through it without fear. Secondly, may we have the right word at the right time that will bring hope and deliverance to those in need. "A word fitly spoken and in due season is like apples of gold in settings of silver" (Proverbs 25:11 AMP). Help us to overcome our self-awareness and become more aware of those sent to us by you, Lord. May we be vessels of honor fit for the Master's use. May the words of our mouths and the meditations of our hearts be pleasing to you oh God. Give us sensitivity to Holy Spirit and His promptings as doors of opportunity open before us daily. In Your Mighty Name and for Your Glory. Amen*

# Dream of Life

Once upon a time, a young woman ran into the restaurant of life. She was in a hurry to choose the best life she could get before rushing out of there, so she asked the server for the easy-to-fix menu. It was stained, well used, and covered with a clouded protective film. It offered a tall stack of unpaid bills, a bring-home-the-bacon minimum wage job, a pie-in-the-sky dream shake, and a banana boat of fluff containing a vacuum-cleaner-salesman surprise and two spoons.

After scanning the easy-to-fix menu, she gave it back to the server and asked for a menu with better choices. She was in a hurry, after all.

This time, she was given the menu of the itinerant chef. The server raved about the chef's creative abilities. Since the young woman wanted to get this life thing going, she happily looked it over. This second menu was upscale, clean, and housed in a black folder. She opened it and was pleased to see no stains, but she grew concerned when she saw no menu choices. Right on cue, the itinerant chef appeared from the kitchen, whisked the menu from her hands, and pointed with pride to the blank pages.

*"Hello, my name is Lackey Direction. I will cook up a house hash that you will love. Just trust me; it will all work out."*

She looked at him warily.

He grinned and said with a wink, *"Just trust me. You will love what I cook up."*

She didn't have a problem with trust—she was from Missouri, after all—but this guy didn't look like a chef to her. More like a grease monkey, a traveling farmhand, or a master imposter. Suddenly, house hash lost all appeal. She knew she wanted more choices.

Tossing the black folder aside, she called for the owner and asked him if there was another menu.

*"We don't use this one much,"* the owner said. *"It's our slow cook menu. We plan the feast, purchase the best ingredients, and start the process, working on every aspect of a five-course meal. We will be happy to serve it you, but you must realize it will take time to accomplish."*

Well, waiting was not her specialty, but the other choices were unacceptable. So she ordered the first course, and the owner prepared it himself. Oh my! If the appetizer was any indication of what was ahead, it would be worth the wait for the entire delicious meal.

All of a sudden, a loud noise rang in my ears. It was the alarm clock. I bolted upright, blinked from the bright sunlight, and remembered the college application lying on my dresser. I thought to myself, *"I think I'll fill that out."*

# What's Growing Underground?

I remember gardening with my grandmother on rocky Missouri soil. My job was to pick up the rocks and throw them over the fence. Each year when the garden was plowed, hoed, and prepared, more Missouri rocks would appear. I knew they didn't grow from weeds or seeds, but it seemed that way. With each cultivation, they rose to the surface, ultimately ending up in my hands to be tossed away.

With the rocks dispatched to the garden's edge, we prepared the rows for planting, making them straight and properly positioned according to what was being sowed. Some crops like green beans, corn, and peas produced edibles above the surface, but other crops bore their fruit below ground, hiding their bounty. These were especially interesting to me because it looked like they were just a bunch of leaves taking up space. Yet, under the surface, produce was growing. Potatoes, beets, onions, carrots, and yams were quietly bringing forth after their kind. It took a while, but at the proper time we would uncover these hidden treasures from the earth, relishing in their nourishment. (Of course, we washed them first.)

Let me encourage you to not judge by what your eyes see, but recognize the distinct possibility of results not readily apparent. Take your prayers, for example. You may see nothing but leaves, but hidden from your natural eyes, the Gardener is working to bring forth what you have prayed. Isaiah tells us,

> *The Spirit of the Lord will rest on him—the Spirit of wisdom and of understanding, the Spirit of counsel and of might, the Spirit of the knowledge and fear of the Lord—and he will delight in the fear of the Lord. He will not judge by what he sees with his eyes, or decide by what he hears with his ears;*

Isaiah 11:2-3

Sometimes our prayers appear to be non-producing, even for America, but there is an underground movement of prayer—a below-the-surface remnant contending for the restoration of biblical values, the preservation of the traditional family, and the demolition of death structures designed to destroy the next generation.

Don't give in to the appearance of unfruitfulness in your prayers. Keep pressing in. Remove the stones, plow through the darkness, and watch the Gardener produce below the surface. Keep tending your garden, knowing there is a season coming when you will see the fruit of your labors.

# It's A Desert Out There

Several years ago, I led a harrowing mission trip to Egypt. This was my first encounter with deserts and quite a paradigm shift for this Missouri girl. We hired a driver to take us through the Sinai to Cairo. As part of the trip, we visited the pyramids at the edge of the Sahara desert. That's when things got interesting. Not only did we get chased by terrorists through the desert, rescued by the Egyptian military, and threatened by fuel pump operators, but I was thrown from a camel and landed in the sand a few inches from a stone wall at the pyramids. You talk about adventure! My children started calling me Indiana Jones. (They claimed Missouri Jones was already taken.)

Enduring two deserts in one trip gave me a picture of life without the modern conveniences of clean food, fresh water, and air conditioning, not to mention cooperative transportation. We are so blessed to live in a beautiful, prosperous country. There are impoverished multitudes throughout the world who believe we are the most privileged creatures to ever walk the planet. Now, I'm not suggesting we send our leftovers in a care package to Egypt. But I am saying that our perspective could improve when it comes to appreciating all we have.

After traveling through Cairo, Luxor, and then Ethiopia, I returned home more appreciative of my comfortable house, my car (not a camel, thank God!), air conditioning, healthy food, and

American prosperity. Sometimes we compare ourselves with those who have more than we do and feel overlooked or slighted in some way. (Why did God bless them more?) Yet compared to the rest of the world, we are, of all peoples, most blessed.

I've decided there is a cure for all the ungrateful, grumpy people living in prosperity. We'll send them on a mission trip to a developing country and see if their hearts change as they encounter poverty-stricken people with scant health care, destitute with little hope for change. Perhaps when they return, the steak that was cooked imperfectly won't irritate them as much. Maybe they won't yell at the waitress who forgot their hot rolls. Or maybe they will begin to care about those around them who have much less than they do.

No, I'm not talking about socialism. I'm talking about caring, sharing, and loving those around us who live in a desert of lack not because they are lazy, but because they find themselves thrown from the supply camel, lying in a desert with no one to help them up. Our ability to help starts with an appreciation for where they are.

# The Open Door Of Opportunity

You never know when the Lord is going to strike—not with lightning but with inspiration from His Spirit.

A friend and I were traveling through Arkansas on our way to a gathering. We talked about many things, enjoying each other's company and looking forward to the meeting. I grew thirsty and headed toward a drive-through for an unsweetened iced tea. (Some people like the sweet kind, but I'm sweet enough without it. Or so people tell me.)

As I approached the drive-through, the Lord told me to reassure the person at the window, saying He had her troubles in mind and was going to take care of her.

His words reverberated through my heart while I continued to talk to my friend. Suddenly, in midsentence, I turned toward the window. There was a young girl taking my money and handing me my tea. I thanked her and asked if I could encourage her. She nodded. I told her, *"The Lord told me to tell you that He is watching over you and to not be concerned about the future."*

She began to cry!

*"What's going on?"* I asked.

She told me of being a single mom with three children, and they would be homeless within two weeks. She poured out her heart at the drive-through window of a fast-food restaurant. Yes, we held up a few cars, although not with a gun but with a prayer line.

I reached out and said, *"Give me your hand."* She took my hand as I prayed for her and her situation. She thanked me for caring enough to tell her what the Lord said, and for praying with her. We took our tea, straws, and lemons and drove away.

Yet here is the icy crunch of this tea story!

My mind argued with the Spirit of God about speaking to this woman before it happened.

First of all, what if I was wrong?

Answer: There is nothing wrong with being wrong.

Secondly, what if I embarrass her?

Answer: A momentary embarrassment will pass, but a word that encourages another person on their journey will last a lifetime.

Thirdly, why do we hesitate to obey the promptings of His Spirit within us?

Answer: We are afraid of being wrong. (See first answer above.)

It was quite a lesson. I was glad to have been used to encourage her.

So we traveled on to our gathering. It was at a nice hotel that had an attendant in the women's restroom. I felt drawn to her. I had lost an earring earlier and asked her to let me know if she found it. Later that day, we talked again about the lost earring. Suddenly, the Lord impressed on me to ask her if there was a man in her life who was going through difficulty. But just as before, my mind argued with the Spirit of the Lord within me. Then I remembered the lessons of the drive-through, and I gathered up my courage to relay the Lord's question to the attendant. Her eyes grew large as she stared at me. She said, *"Yes, my brother lives on the streets and is mentally ill. We haven't heard from him for several years."*

I replied, *"Do you mind if we pray for him?"* She reached out her hand and we agreed in prayer for her brother's wellbeing. After the prayer, she smiled and thanked me for taking the time to care about her. I knew God had made an impact on her life.

Here is the key to obeying the Lord's still small voice. Let your focus be on the person who needs encouragement about their situation. It's not what people think of us, or what we look like or sound like that matters. Take the opportunities that appear before you. Risk, step out in faith, and assist someone in their journey through life.

# Purposeful Living

What is the goal?

Sometimes our goal is to just get through the day. I remember my grandmother telling me her favorite song was "One Day at a Time." She was a widow at age 50 with nine children, seven of whom were still living at home. She managed to raise them well. She never remarried or learned to drive a car. But she lived to be 90 years old. She lived through 40 years without her husband, raising their children, managing a farm, and living life one day at a time.

But, as admirable as that is, living one day at a time cannot be our only goal.

What is the goal?

I believe it's called *purpose*. Every person born on this earth comes with a purpose to fulfill. Yet many of us live life without ever finding that purpose. Sure, there are pursuits that occupy our time, jobs that keep us busy, and family that brings us joy, but purpose still eludes us. When I talk with someone who has spent their life ignoring their dreams, thinking they are unattainable, I see a person who has not attained their purpose. The Lord has written a destiny inside each one of us—a dream to be walked out.

David tells us about that reality:

> *My frame was not hidden from you when I was made in the secret place, when I was woven together in*

*the depths of the earth. Your eyes saw my unformed body; all the days ordained for me were written in your book before one of them came to be. How precious to me are your thoughts, God! How vast is the sum of them!*

Psalm 139:15-17

Those days ordained and planned for us were written before we were born. How exciting is that! Why am I here? That question has an answer. It's found in your relationship with Jesus Christ. He knew you before you were born. He set you on this earth to make a difference. He put dreams in your heart, gave you breath, and watches over you to bring fulfillment. Of course, we all have a choice to go our own way, and many do. Unfulfilled dreams make unfulfilled people! But it's never too late. Destiny can be delayed but not denied. The Lord is gracious to get us back on track when we ask.

*Ask and it will be given to you; seek and you will find; knock and the door will be opened to you.*

Matthew 7:7

Find your purpose, walk out your destiny, and live in the joy of knowing who you are and why you exist.

# IV

# LOSS

*Father of Spirits,*

*We call upon you today to Father us. You created us in your image, after your likeness. Your word says that we have a High Priest who is able to understand and sympathize and have shared feelings with our weaknesses and infirmities. You know what we are going through, and you care. In every trial, in every loss, may you surround us with your grace. May you heal our wounded hearts. Thank you for assuring us of eternal life through Jesus Christ and His death on the cross. Fill the empty spaces in our hearts with your love, your comfort, and your presence. When we walk through the valley of the shadow of death, you are with us. Help us to process our losses with your help. Restore what can be restored in this life and give us assurance of restoration with our loved ones in eternity. Thank you for your grace, comfort, and peace. Amen*

# The Orange Butterfly

*The sun shone brightly as I drove to the cemetery.*
*I knew she was not there, but I had to check.*
*Mom died suddenly without warning*
*And my heart was heavy with loss.*
*"Lord, talk to me. I need some reassurance.*

*I'm a believer. Yet, death seems so final. Are you here?*
*Where is Mom? She's not in that grave; I just know it.*
*Help me process this grief. Help me see this from a different view.*
*Your view."*

The cemetery was empty of life when I arrived. Wilted flowers lay strewn across the fresh grave. Mom's was in the same plot as my brother's. Even though his had been there a long time, the old pain still surfaced. At only age 19, he was taken from this life.

I prayed again as I walked toward the graves. Just as I finished praying, a small orange butterfly began hovering over my head. It came closer, circling me like I was its prey. It had no fear of me, nor did it seem to notice when I moved away. It followed hard after me as if on a mission, finally landing on my shoulder and remaining there for quite some time. It slowly beat its wings, spreading them out, then bringing them back together as if to say, *"See my wings!"*

Suddenly the Lord spoke to my heart, *"I am the resurrection and the life. Death is only the cocoon that leads us to resurrection. It is costly to die, but there is life after death, and your mother is with me. By the way, she loves her new body, and she is learning to fly."*

The tears began to flow and trust returned to my heart. The orange butterfly left my shoulder, appearing translucent in the sun as it flitted off to display God's glory elsewhere.

A year later, my father passed away. My sister and I were able to lead him to the Lord before he died. We sat at his funeral on a warm day, his ashes displayed before us on a small pedestal against a backdrop of large windows. As the military guard finished the salute, my eyes were drawn to a small orange butterfly outside the windows, flitting its glory through the glass and displaying a familiar message to my heart.

The message was clear; there is life after death. The seeming finality of death's blow was lifted off my heart as I recognized the transformation of a small creature. In the destiny of a worm lay the potential to fly above the earth and take on, not only the beauty of the butterfly, but the ability to soar above earth's gravity. The transformation took place in the cocoon of death. Emerging from its grip, the worm was transformed. Jesus was the first to conquer death, conquering its grip. He did it for all of us .

> *The heavens declare the glory of God; the skies proclaim the work of his hands. Day after day they pour forth speech; night after night they reveal knowledge. They have no speech, they use no words; no sound is heard from them. Yet their voice goes out into all the earth, their words to the ends of the world. In the heavens God has pitched a tent for the sun.*
>
> Psalm 19:1-4

# The Funeral Train

*Left to find reason or rhyme,*
*The moving, mourning train releases the pent-up vapor*
*Of unpredictable anguish*
*In the form of patterned performance of duties*
*Brought on by the death of a family member.*

*Moving on track previously laid*
*By generations of funeral makers,*
*The train enters the dark tunnel of memorial's dwelling place.*
*Darkened by death's unexpected intrusion,*
*The tunnel hollows out a place for itself in the landscape of*
*forgotten routine.*
*How can a moving train slow its pace to a stop*
*To allow its occupants time to lie on the side of the road*
*To weep for the loss of life so precious.*

*There are few stops for this train.*
*It moves on schedule, engineered to lumber through stop after stop*
*Of choice upon choice, until flower after flower*
*Wilts in its place in the sun,*
*And the once vibrant living one is brought to the end of the tunnel.*
*The train roars to a stop.*
*The lonely whistle blows "Amazing Grace."*
*The occupants detrain.*
*The grass on the side of the road waves an invitation.*
*Face down in clovered green,*

*Sidetracked train passengers finger their ticket stubs,*
*Trying to touch what is missing.*
*Brief relief releases its moment to grief,*
*As the clouds of stormy pain release rain*
*On the grass beside the road.*
*This train ride is over.*
*The track goes on to carry the train to its next destination.*
*Distant relatives and brief acquaintances,*
*Bored at this stop, board the train that carries*
*The next group of pained passengers.*

# Where Were You?

We were in Israel on a prayer trip when 9-11 hit America. You don't forget significant life-changing events like that. We were traveling down the mountain that overlooked the Valley of Jezreel when we got a call on one of the cellphones from a contact in Israel. She gave us the news that America was under attack. Each of us wanted to reach our family in America as soon as possible to make sure they were ok, but the circuits were jammed and we couldn't get through. To complicate matters, one of my sons was in Germany on tour with a band and was also trying to get in touch with his dad in America.

Unable to contact our loved ones, we drove up to Elijah's cave, went inside, and prayed long for our nation. No one was sure what would happen next. Israel promptly closed the airport. Flights in and out of Tel Aviv were halted. Would Israel be the next target? We contemplated taking a boat to Cyprus, but chose instead to wait it out where we were. We returned to our hotel and watched the horrifying video of the attack.

Life changes so quickly. One minute we are secure; the next minute our lives are turned upside down. What do you do in a situation like that?

First, don't let fear take over. Fear comes with a lot of "what ifs."

- What if we can't get home?
- What if Israel is next?
- What if they don't open the airport for weeks?
- What if...?

Second, don't panic or make rash decisions. Listen to wise counsel. Unless you are in known danger, take your time and make rational decisions. This is what we tried to do.

Third, wait it out. In a few hours, the phone lines to America were available and we were able to contact our families. The Lord gives grace to walk through difficult circumstances.

After a week or so, the Tel Aviv airport opened and we rescheduled our flights home. Security was indescribable. They went through everything with a fine-tooth comb. We were grateful because we wanted to be safe, but the process took forever. Finally, we boarded the plane and lifted off. They closed the airport immediately after our flight. We had been given a small window to get out and we made it.

Arriving at the airport in the USA, I was so thankful to be home that I wanted to kiss the ground. As we went through the arrival gates, one of the agents turned our way with a welcoming grin and asked, "Where have you cowboys and cowgirls been?" I wanted to hug that guy! We were home. My love for America had grown by leaps and bounds. I wanted to embrace my nation, but my arms weren't big enough. I wanted to look into the eyes of each person who had been damaged by this attack and bring some kind of hope to them. Instead, with my eyes brimming with tears, I went to collect my luggage.

None of us would ever be the same again.

# Dealing with Loss

I loved my Mother's Day present from our daughter and her family; it was a beautiful hibiscus tree in full bloom. I tenderly replanted it in a larger pot and set smaller flowers and sweet potato vines in the soil around its base. We placed it on our back deck and enjoyed the flowering beauty. A few days later, after a brief trip to Texas, I discovered some creature had eaten all the hibiscus leaves from the branches and also devoured the leaves from my sweet potato vine. I was heartsick.

I think because it was a gift from our daughter, its sentimental value was greater than its replacement value. What does that mean? It simply means it hurt my heart. Something beautiful that I cherished had been destroyed by an unseen animal with no ability to care how its actions affected me. The tender leaves were merely a salad supper for some being of nature. (My only consolation was knowing my ranch dressing, bacon bits, and tomatoes were still in the refrigerator.) Yes, this was a small loss in the grand scheme of life, but great for its sentimental value. I had to process grief, anger, frustration, and helplessness. And then I had to clean up the mess.

Loss affects us deeply, doesn't it? I have experienced worse losses than a gobbled hibiscus tree, and all of them take time to process. When I lost my brother many years ago, strong emotions gripped me: regret, sorrow, pain, depression, and hopelessness. Working through loss takes time, but it's important to walk it out, talk it out, and process it through. The alternative—stuffing emotions down inside us—can be detrimental to our health. This is why Jesus said, "Cast your cares on me."

But how do we do that? How do we cast our cares on Him?

We start by speaking it out. For example: *"Lord, I give you these emotions of hurt, pain, and anger. I give you this situation. You are the only one who can carry me through this. I choose to give it to you. Fill this empty place with your love and grace."* Keep releasing your emotions until you begin to feel better. The key is to get it out and not let it impact your emotional or physical health. Don't isolate. Talk to the Lord and find trusted friends to help you process.

Remember, we walk *through* the valley; we don't *live* there.

# Regaining What Was Lost

Ever wish you could return to the innocence of days gone by? When family values were the standard and everyone knew what a traditional family looked like? When people sat on their porches in the evening and neighbors strolled over for a visit, sharing homemade lemonade and conversation about friends and family? Unfortunately, returning to yesteryear is not possible apart from classic movies, books, and television. Technology has transformed relationship, and media has supplanted the simple art of entertaining friends. We now text instead of talk. And Facebook is the place to go for information, opinions, and occasional rants, replacing the coffee klatches and backyard fence conversations of a bygone era.

To be clear, technology alone doesn't bother me. As I write this, I'm working on a laptop and planning to email it to my editor. No, technology is only the means of information sharing. My issue is with the content—television producers and network owners saturating our lives with their brand of culturally-influenced entertainment produced by agenda-driven groups seeking to transform society.

Let's face it! It's difficult to tune into any media—television, radio, internet—without encountering offensive scenes and dialog. Call me old-fashioned if you like, but our family values are being slowly eroded by the torrent of sepsis released into our daily lives. This stream of toxic, sexually-explicit, aberrant behavior is destroying not only the innocence of our children but the traditional family as well.

Is anyone out there concerned about the lack of covenant relationship in today's world? The descending number of church goers in our nation? The diminishing numbers of those who embrace the Bible as the standard for living? If things get bad enough, perhaps the "silent majority" will become the awakened "vocal majority."

No, we don't have to go back to yesteryear—indeed, we cannot—but we must restore the structures and principles that made America great. We cannot lose the nourishing environment of family arising from one husband married to one wife, raising children who have both a mother and a father. Nor can we bear to lose families who are committed to each other, demonstrating long-term commitment through marriage and caring about the legacy they are leaving for their children and grandchildren.

Yes, I know it is not possible to live in a perfect world, but God did establish the structure of family in His Word. In my opinion, it has not lost its value. The Lord loves all of us where we are, but He has established safe structures of growth and stability for mankind. I mean no condemnation here, just a heart-plea for the restoration of Godly values and the structure of the family that provides a loving environment for a healthy future.

# Make A Joyful Noise

I love the sound of musical instruments. The blast of the trumpet reaches my heart and draws me out to experience awakening. The flute is light and cheerful, bringing memories of forests and creeks. The saxophone reminds me of an elephant's trunk when it is lifted up in the wind. It has a masculine sound that adds depth to an orchestration and puts the jazz in Jazz. The sweet violin is so versatile; depending on its mood, it can make us dance, weep, or hear the wind in the willows.

I love them all.

The guitar was popularized by American cowboy movies, blues singers, and rock bands starting in the 50's, becoming indispensable to our favorite crooners. Today, it is a vital part of Christian worship bands. Many churches have moved from organs and pianos to a band with multiple instruments. Yet keyboard instruments still move me.

Music was created for us to enjoy! Music produces a response in the hearer. Plug your voice into the mix and experience a shift in your musical paradigm.

The Bible tells us to make a joyful noise, so even if you don't play an instrument, you can still sing. Nobody said it had to be on pitch. Of course, if you are leading worship, you'll need some skill. But joined with fellow believers or alone in your car, even a screeching sound can be a joyful noise. So don't stop; it is good for the soul.

Psalm 57 directs us to awake harp and lyre, sing in the dawn. I remember going through a difficult time years ago; the last thing I wanted to do was sing. Yet, I felt the Lord directing me to do so. He knew if I would open my mouth and sing, even when I didn't feel like it, my soul would follow along and come out of its despair. The scripture specifically says to sing in the dawn. Dawn represents breakthrough. When dawn comes, darkness fades away. I took that advice to heart and sang in my breakthrough.

The Lord is worthy of worship even when we don't feel like it. Get out that instrument and play it. Yes, your voice is an instrument. Make a joyful noise! Sing! Play! You will produce a pleasant response—I guarantee it—first in you and then in those around you.

# V

# QUIETNESS

*Lord,*

*I ask you to quiet my noisy heart. Cause me to be still and know that you are God. I choose today to cast my cares on you because you care for me because I know you are able to orchestrate victory on my behalf. Forgive me for my anxious thoughts and my worrisome attitude toward life and it's trials. I lay it all at your feet, asking you to calm my fears and release me from the grip of fear. I choose to rest from my labors and enter into the resting place of your Presence. I tell my heart to believe again, to hope again, to trust again. In quietness and confidence, I reach out to find my resting place in you. I choose to be still, knowing you are watching over my life as the shepherd of my soul. Have your way in me. Amen*

# Wisdom Waits

For some reason, I don't do well with loudness—noisy restaurants, clamorous talking sirens, clanging bells, or screaming children. All of this tends to bother me. My husband has learned to mute the television during commercials, and when he isn't home, he knows I will mute the sound of an entire program and read the dialog. I'm sure this isn't "normal." I'm also sure it's because I am with people much of the day and at the end of it, I am ready for peace and quiet.

I like to quiet my heart, silencing the clanging gong of life and finding that place of peace within. I don't think its weirdness; I think it's healthy. Unless we find a place of rest, we live lives filled with yesterday's static projected into today's challenges.

Some keys to erasing static include forgiveness—releasing problems and relationship issues to the Lord, asking for His wisdom, and seeking refuge in His Word and Presence. I wrote the following to illustrate the daily challenge we face to turn off the noise of life and hear the quiet, profound voice of Jesus. Perhaps you can relate.

## Heart At Rest

*Rest created, outwardly found,*
*Loses its grip when sound comes around.*
*Gongs and bells, whistles and yells,*
*Pound at the door where sanctum dwells.*
*Quickly ignored, yet constantly crashing,*
*Like waves of thunder and lightning flashing.*
*The sound continues with none to subdue it,*
*None to command it, few to temper it.*
*It stages itself, performing at will,*
*Refusing to yield or honor the still.*

*Wisdom waits quietly outside the door,*
*But refuses to enter while noise has the floor.*
*Lurking outside like a vagrant unwanted,*
*He waits for his moment steadfastly undaunted.*
*With treasures untapped, keys not yet given,*
*He longs to deposit the sweet wealth of Heaven.*
*He searches for one whose rest is within,*
*One who has conquered the invasive din.*
*With rest created and inwardly found,*
*Wisdom will enter and find fertile ground.*

# Run, Run, Run

*Duty chases and culture beckons.*
*Bullies follow and pressure threatens.*
*Are you running from or running to?*
*Winning the race or just passing through?*
*Your heart beats fast as your feet pound stone.*
*Will you ever be through to find your way home?*

*Run Run, Run!*
*Time never stops as seconds keep burning.*
*Tyrants are chasing and fear shoots its warning.*
*There's no time for rest, not even for breathing.*
*Joy of life stands on the sidelines waiting.*
*The quiet place is an empty womb.*
*Drums of demand beat an ominous gloom.*

*Someday I'll stop and sit for a while,*
*Rocking my chair and sporting a smile.*
*Reflecting on trials of a far busy life,*
*And regretting the race that once stole my life.*
*What was the prize I was hoping to gain?*
*What part of success would've been my refrain?*

*Time moved on and so did I.*
*My feet walked the walk while time chose to fly.*
*Now that I know what I didn't know then,*
*My heart would return to who knows when.*

*But time flew in to steal the day*
*And marched right through the month of May.*
*Refusing to stop and seize the day,*
*It balked at the thought of any delay.*
*No tickets were offered to yesterday!*

*What have I gained from running so fast?*
*Nothing of substance, none that will last.*
*I built my plan and achieved the best.*
*From the human viewpoint, I was a success.*
*But beauty unnoticed and songs unsung,*
*Drew me to seek the Greater One.*

*Was there a plan I could have found?*
*One that carried a melodious sound,*
*Of peace and rest in spite of my goals?*
*Of treasured moments and helpful roles?*

*I heard the gentle breath of rest,*
*Whisper to my beating breast.*
*Your written destiny still waits.*
*Slow my child and work your best!*

*In repentance and rest is your salvation,*
*In quietness and trust is your strength.*

Isaiah 30:15

# The Color Of Joy

I love painting with words. It is challenging but it can be done.

So what color would you use to paint a picture of joy?

Red won't do. It is the color of murder scenes, fire trucks, and emergency beacons. Combined with orange, it is the fire itself.

Blue is worth a try. Maybe the news isn't out yet, but it was recently disqualified by the color guard for hanging out on a street corner last Monday "singing the blues."

Green is the color of life: grass, leaves, evergreens, baking apples, green beans. Still, mold is green and who wants that?

Yellow might be a good choice; it brings thoughts of sunshine, buttercups, canaries, banana taffy. But there's also yellow jaundice, yellow fever, and cowards!

Painting a word picture of joy is harder than I thought. Let's throw all the colors together in a container to see if we come up with joy. According to the American Museum of Natural History, "White light is a combination of all colors in the color spectrum. It has all the colors of the rainbow. Combining primary colors like red, blue, and green creates secondary colors: yellow, cyan, and magenta. All other colors can be broken down into different combinations of three primary colors." Hmmm…does that sound like joy?

It appears that objects are the color of the light they reflect. I want to reflect joy, even if I don't know what color it is. So what is joy?

Joy is bouncy like a ball, internal rather than external, a fruit of the Spirit (Galatians 5:22), produced in the presence of the Lord (Psalm 16:11). Joy gives us strength (Nehemiah 8:10), spreading its sweetness like jelly on the bread of life. Superficial laughter is not joy. Happiness can be a momentary respite from the trials of life, but joy has staying power. Its essence lingers throughout the day and gives us strength to rise above circumstances that could otherwise destroy inner strength.

Too bad we only sing "Joy to the World" at Christmas. Here's my version of a year-round ode to joy.

### Spectrum

*Shallow laughter born of pain*
*Meant to mask a lonely strain*
*Remits its sound of brief relief*
*A quick escape from pain and grief.*

*The can of laughter vents its spray*
*Tinting life with shades of gray.*
*The parlor light grows dimmer still*
*As morning colors crest the hill.*

*Melting off the tallowed brine*
*Glorious light begins to shine.*
*Opening to joys unknown*
*I find my rest before His Throne.*

*Though you have not seen him, you love him, and even though you do not see him now, you believe in him and are filled with an inexpressible and glorious joy.*

I Peter 1:8

76

# Memory's Moments

As you think back on life, are there moments you would like to relive? Most of us would probably not choose our turbulent teenage years, but a more joyful time—the arrival of a child, a favorite vacation, graduating from college or landing our first job. Moments cannot be relived but they can be cherished forever through memory. Our five senses take in the fragrance, touch, taste, sounds, and sights of life's journey and file them away. Because moments are fleeting, they must be captured within and occasionally allowed out for others to share. After we reminisce, they must be tucked away again along with Grandma's handmade doilies and quilts in the cedar chest of sentiment's cache. I tried to capture the essence of the process in this poem. I hope you enjoy it.

# The River

*A moment comes but never stays.*
*It swiftly moves with no delays.*
*Future moments loom ahead*
*But moments past are never dead.*
*Moments come and moments go.*
*They never linger, only flow.*
*Like a river never stops*
*Moments trickle past the rocks*
*Of birth and death and mortal lives*
*Rarely seen by human eyes.*
*Slipped through fingers like the sand*
*So is lost the plans of man.*
*Yet memories will never fade*
*Living in the soul's arcade.*
*Life moves fast yet leaves behind*
*The cherished drops of precious time.*
*Of growth and play and love's array*
*Of pain and joy and quiet days.*
*Though moments flee like rivers flow*
*All are captured in my soul.*

# VI

# RELATIONSHIPS

*Lord Jesus,*

*Purify my heart. Keep me free from hatred, hurt, revenge, and selfish ways. Help me to find the way behind the wall of hurt and offense to reach the hurting hearts of others. When I am misunderstood or misjudged, help me respond and not react. When my life is damaged by unrighteous ways and angry words, help me remember the path of life is through forgiveness and release of offense. Offenses come, but they don't have to stay. I will not embrace them, but release them to you. I have been forgiven, so I choose to forgive. I thank you that my choice is stronger than my feelings. I choose to love, not because it is deserved, but because it is necessary and right. I refuse to live with a bitter heart, offended heart, so cleanse me fresh and new from past painful experiences and keep my heart soft toward You and others. Amen*

# Walking The Tightrope

Whose side are you on, anyway? Never a pleasant question.

Recently I've had the opportunity to be the sounding board for two parties on either side of a disagreement over perception and direction. Being the peacemaker requires both tact and wisdom. Thankfully it wasn't a political altercation. Actually, it wasn't an altercation at all, but a difference of opinion brought on through relationship conflict. Not knowing all the facts or the path that brought them to this impasse caused severe navigational difficulties. Yet, as a friend to both parties, I was willing to listen.

Have you ever been put in a similar situation, knowing you had to tiptoe through the tulips lest you crush them? How do you say what needs to be said without causing more conflict, hurt, or damage? Of course, that's a rhetorical question. (For those who skipped English class that day, *rhetorical* means it's a question without an expected answer.) When each party talked with me, they weren't expecting an immediate solution. Instead, they both wanted a listening ear and an understanding heart—in a word: *validation.* Eventually, each person separately asked my opinion and counsel, and I was able to help.

Because the Lord has allowed me to walk through difficult situations in life, I had no reprimands, criticisms or platitudes to spout to either party. I'd been where they were, knew the territory, and got the T-shirt. Conflict navigation can be a circus with the mediator as the tightrope walker. So began my painstaking journey of helping them bridge the valley of misunderstanding.

Walking the narrow road to mutual understanding brought us to the reality of false perceptions and wounded hearts. Simple, rhetorical questions brought results as each person settled their emotions and assumed a teachable heart.

When faced with daunting challenges, I often prepare by asking myself how much I really know. Invariably, the answer is, "Not much!" This reminds me to remain teachable in any situation, enabling me to bring growth and resolution to any conflict.

Of course, I don't always get it right. None of us do. Our perspectives on most any situation will differ because of personality, background, wounds or experience. Several years ago, a wise woman said to me, "If both of us agree all the time, one of us is unnecessary." I'm not sure I agree totally with that statement because I do see the need for different perspectives regarding any situation because each of us sees only a portion. When we add our portion to that of others, we get a more complete picture.

Even some insects have compound eyes, as described in this paragraph: "If you've stalked six-legged pests and been frustrated by how tricky it is to get the jump on them, here's why: you can't sneak up on insects. No matter which direction you're coming from, they can see you and take evasive action. Their bulging convex eyes, each containing thousands of mini-eyes, give bugs wraparound vision." (http://animals.mom.me)

The Bible says in I Corinthians that we see in a mirror dimly, so perhaps adding the perspective of another person could give us a clearer picture. Food for thought, and bread and butter in relationships.

# Great Gardening

Surveying the tiny dots the size of pinheads, I marveled at their potential. Really? These little grains of nothing are going to become large, colorful, and beautiful? How can this be? The package came with the usual instructions: plant, water, illuminate. With proper care and a little plant food, the blooming flowers would come forth as advertised. Well, these dots certainly didn't possess any of the vibrant colors promised on the package. Yet these small seeds contained all the ingredients to fulfill their ultimate potential of beautifying the earth and releasing their fragrance into my space.

Now, suppose those seeds represent a person's potential. And suppose it doesn't appear the person will ever be what they were meant to be. But suppose he or she never had the proper care to grow, mature, and display the beautiful plan of God for their lives. And maybe, just maybe…we could stretch this analogy a little further and see the soil as the love of God and the water as His cleansing. If we tried really hard, we could see the intended beauty set to burst forth.

So what keeps it from happening? Maybe the weeds and thorns of life are choking the seedling and hindering its growth. Maybe the garden needs to be tended by someone who can see the picture of a joyful, released, loved person. Maybe that person is you?

The church is a greenhouse for seedlings who desperately need a gardener—one who tenderly cares for plants that others would throw away. If we could see the potential planted in each person, perhaps we would not be so quick to judge their outward appearance. Because we are in the employ of the Gardener, our job is to visualize the end result and assist in its outcome.

> *The righteous will flourish like a palm tree, they will grow like a cedar of Lebanon; planted in the house of the Lord, they will flourish in the courts of our God.*

Psalm 92:12-13

# Bigotry

I'm not sure I understand the term *bigotry* as it is sometimes applied. It seems that those of us who believe in a standard taught by God's Word are portrayed by those with no standard (save their own perceptions) as judgmental bigots. I submit that we are labeled such, not because we deserve it, but because a Biblical standard does not agree with our accuser's behavior or lifestyle.

> *In English, the word "bigot" refers to a prejudiced, closed-minded person who is intolerant or hateful toward people of a different group, especially racial or religious.*

> Wikipedia

Based on this definition, attitudes toward others that breed hatred fit the definition of bigotry. The closed-minded aspect of bigotry speaks of being unteachable and shut off from truth. These isolationist attitudes could very well leave one in a delusional state. Certainly, freedom of choice is still valid both in America and in God's Word. We are free to choose our way. Without this freedom, dictatorships take over, tyranny rises, and freedom loses. We must have freedom to make our own choices on all sides of any issue. But those choices *do* have consequences.

Boundaries set by the Word of God are there for our protection, not to deny our freedom but to protect it from our destructive ways.

There is great freedom within the boundaries of love. I do not have to love a person's behavior or lifestyle to love that person. I did not love the behavior of my two-year-old son when he defiantly threw his peas on the floor, but I still loved my son.

I suspect the perspective of true bigots is so skewed that they believe anyone with a differing viewpoint is judgmental. For my part, any lifestyle that is destructive to me, my family, or our freedom will not be tolerated. This does not make me intolerant. It makes me wise. So, for any true bigots out there, don't accuse me out of your own guilt. Take off the clouded glasses of offense and respect my belief system—the Word of God that has and always will protect us from the destructive results of wrong decisions. At the same time, you are free to choose your own way, however destructive it might be.

Even destructive behavior is wiped away by the sacrifice of Jesus as we humbly come to Him admitting our need of forgiveness and allowing Him to change our hearts.

# Willful Sleeper

*Awake, you who choose to dream*
*Who choose to rest in your own realm.*
*Lulled by decades of lullaby lyrics*
*And years of tightening mind grips*
*Oblivious to a reality an awakening away.*

*Your sleeping room is adorned with diminishing décor.*
*With each breath drawn in solemn slumber*
*Reality grows smaller and smaller until*
*All awareness of wakefulness vanishes into vanity.*

*This downward fall into sleep's stall seems pleasant to the senses*
*For in this realm, you are the helmsman*
*Steering the soul of self-service on the stained-glass sea*
*Fragmented and shattered by grips of pain.*

*Hopelessly trapped in sleep's habitat, you long for a glimpse of*
*true dimension.*
*Shallow facades and two-sided figures float sadly stilted*
*And staged through this land of settled dogma.*
*Through land and sea, you sleep aimlessly, restlessly gaining no*
*awareness.*

*Pressed into this headless bed, you sleep your chosen victimhood*
*Being vexed by fear, frightened by feelings, and frozen into*
*friendless frenzy.*

Chosen sleep cannot be disrupted nor can delusions
Be broken by alarming words.
The knobs of willful and chosen tune out the
Rising tide of emergency sirens sounding
In rescue and routed by pleas of the awakened.

Sip this conclusion from your cup as you sit at your morning table.
It isn't the awakener who fails in his task to shake the beds of self-
choosing.
Will upon will have been piled upon the still
And haven't grown worn from the using.

Awake, you who choose to dream,
You who choose to rest in your own realm,
From the land of reality, the awakened long
To reach your beating heart before it vanishes into vanity,
Before its corridors are cut off from the cry of another's hope.

Awaken! Awaken! Reality awaits.

# VII

# FAITH

*Father,*

*Your Word says that faith is a substance, yet it cannot be seen with the natural eyes. It's like the wind because we can see its result, but cannot see the substance of it. I thank you that faith is strong enough to uproot structures of death and disease. It is strong enough to change a river's course and transform a person's life. Faith can be a gift, so I ask you for the gift of faith to believe for the impossible, to believe for the supernatural. You created the world and everything in it. You set its systems in place. You said that life and death are in the power of the tongue, so cause me to speak what you are speaking. You said that the eyes of our heart can be enlightened, so cause me to see with the eyes of my heart what you are seeing. Keep me from misplaced faith: faith in my own strength rather than yours, faith in the things of this life instead of the substance of heaven. Lord, I agree with the prayer you taught your disciples, may your Kingdom come and your will be done on this earth as it is done in heaven. Once again, I ask for the gift of faith. In the Name that is above every Name, Jesus.*

*Amen*

# Believe, Hope, Sit, Trust

I heard someone say the other day that she didn't have faith. She was wrong, of course. Everyone has faith. Whenever you sit in a chair, you assume the chair will hold you up. That's faith. It is simply the belief in something or someone.

The problem comes as our faith is tested and our expectations shatter to the floor. Broken faith comes when we put our hope in something or someone who did not come through for us. When we choose to trust someone or something, we have an expectation of fulfillment. For instance, you expected the chair to resist the gravitational pull of the earth on your behalf (or behind, as the case may be). Perhaps you sat in that same chair every day for five years. Your expectations were high and your faith grew exponentially until there was no doubt the chair will hold you up. Until the day the legs snapped and you crashed to the floor.

So...are you never sitting in a chair again? That would be absurd! Yet, I've heard people make similar statements. "I'll never trust anyone again!" Obviously, not all chairs are unstable, nor are all people.

Perhaps your faith in mankind has been tested. Some people are wobbly as old chairs. Others are stable as rocks. However, people *in general* aren't the problem. It's particular people who can be a problem. Let's face it: trust is earned! But to form a judgment about all people or all chairs severely limits your relational options and/or physical comfort.

Hello! Wisdom calling! Don't judge the future by the past. And don't put your trust in wobbly people. Faith is a trust that develops over time through experiences proving the integrity of an object or person. The Bible says it this way,

> *Faith is the substance of things hoped for, the evidence of things not seen.*

Hebrews 11:1(NKJV)

Believe me: one unworthy chair shouldn't cause you to empty your house of all furniture. Likewise, don't empty your life of relationships after one or two fail you. Instead, believe again, hope again, sit again, and trust the Lord always. He is faithful when others are not.

Maybe the problem that felled you wasn't a chair at all, but a maintenance issue. Maintaining our spiritual relationship with the Lord keeps us from falling. He preserves our faith and trust intact.

# Comfort Zone

Comfort is a valued, marketable item. Few people sleep without a comfortable pillow; few people walk without comfortable shoes. In winter, we have heat; in summer, we have air conditioning. But it goes much further. We often live our lives settled in a comfortable place. It's interesting to watch elderly people nestled in their comfortable chair surrounded by the TV remote, the box of Kleenex, their half-finished book, a glass of tea, and a paper plate with their favorite half-eaten brownie.

There is nothing wrong with comfort until you grow roots and refuse to move out of it, even when opportunity knocks on your door. One reason we stay in our comfortable place is fear. Comfortable places are safe places. Stepping out of our comfort zone can be challenging.

When someone is doing extremely well in some activity, we say they are *in the zone*. The online slang dictionary defines *in the zone* as: *Achieving an unheard-of level of performance*. Notice that the comfort zone does not allow for such achievement. It is the antithesis of high performance. Our challenge is to go beyond the norm, outside the familiar, and expand our present horizon.

Consider Peter who was willing to leave the comfort of the boat at the command of Jesus despite a raging storm. Consider Benjamin Franklin who flew a kite in a storm to explore electricity. Daily, we reap the benefit of his bold, dangerous venture.

How far are you willing to venture beyond your achievable, tangible comfort? Does your adventure end with a TV remote? Have your dreams settled into an easy chair? Are you really living or just going through the motions?

I know it's challenging, but tap into those dreams again; face your fears head-on and step out of the comfort zone to live *in the zone*—an unheard-of level of performance. It's within you to live the abundant life. Go for it!

# Overcoming Fear

I love adventure—new people, new places, new cultures. Pioneering original things challenges and energizes me. I enjoy driving through small towns and exploring unknown territory. Given the choice, I'll take America's back roads over interstates any day. The last time I took a team to Bosnia, we chose to find our way around without a guide or interpreter. The connecting pastor was shocked. (We *did* have a cellphone to reach him, just in case.) I have also led teams to Russia, China, Romania, Hungary, Italy, Ethiopia, Egypt, Croatia, and Honduras. I'm not afraid to embrace novel opportunities, engage strangers, interact with foreign cultures or even start businesses.

But I haven't always been adventurous. For many years, I was unwilling to leave my comfort zone, afraid to travel to unknown places, and reluctant to start new entities. I remember sitting in high school English class knowing the answers but afraid to speak because my words might not come out right. Fear was my constant companion, so I hid behind a silent facade. Instead of engaging with the world and everyone in it, I fought an internal battle with fear. Ironically, it was the fear of rejection that reinforced my isolation from people. Yet inside, the real me was yearning to emerge.

So what happened between high school and now? The healing power of Jesus' love—that's what happened. He changed me. 1John 4:18 says, "There is no fear in love. But perfect love drives out fear, because fear has to do with punishment. The one who fears is not made perfect in love." The love of the Father through His Son Jesus Christ began to invade my life, uprooting fear and rejection, releasing me from isolation, causing me to emerge from my shell and engage the abundant, exciting world around me. I realized I was totally loved and accepted even in my fear-filled condition. This loving acceptance displaced the foundation of fear in my life.

It's true—perfect love *does* cast out fear. I've experienced it. If you battle with fear, ask the Father to allow you to experience His perfect love through Jesus Christ. It's the perfect antidote for fear.

# Faux Pas In Egypt

I like to enter new doors, explore new places, meet new people, dine at mom and pop restaurants, drive through small towns, visit foreign nations, experience other cultures, and generally expand my horizons. The good things in life are meant to be experienced, right? But sometimes you can get more than planned. I remember an unforgettable experience from entering a wrong portal.

On a mission trip to Egypt several years ago, we dined at an outdoor restaurant in Cairo with our team and hired driver. At the end of the meal, I had to find a women's restroom. Since I couldn't read Arabic, I was a bit handicapped in my search. Our driver pointed me to an open door a few feet away, so I entered it. (Remember that I like to enter new doors?) Wrong move! It was a restroom all right, but it was full of Egyptian men in Middle Eastern garb. They all turned and stared dumbfounded at me. I was an intrusive guest.

Realizing my mistake, I quickly turned, found my way to the women's facilities *inside* the restaurant, and returned to our table confident that I'd covered my tracks. I was about to rejoin the conversation when, out of the corner of my eye, I saw activity at the threshold of the men's facility. The men were throwing a bucket of soapy water on the steps and floor of the entrance. Confused, I shared my brief adventure with the team. The Egyptian guide explained that the men had to cleanse the threshold because a woman had entered it. This was more than an *oops!* or a faux pas. It was a cultural offense. I, as an American woman–or any woman, for that matter—was *forbidden* to pass through that door.

Wishing to avoid an international incident, we gathered our things and paid the bill. On the way back to our van, one of our team members, a young man, got sick at his stomach. He could not hold it any longer and so deposited everything into the flower pot beside the same door that had just been scrubbed. We put our heads down and kept walking.

Lessons from this exploit:

- Don't walk through wrong doors, especially in Egypt.

- Be careful what you eat in a foreign country.

- After cultural faux pas, disappear into the crowd as quickly as possible.

- After you get to safety, instruct your team to do as you *say,* not as you *do.*

- Write a book about an American missionary team and their stomach issues in Egypt

- Remember, not every open door should be entered.

- Run, Forest! Run!

# Peaches And Prayer

My favorite fruit is a peach. It is so warm and fuzzy, especially when picked from the orchard in the early morning sun. When you peel back the fuzzy skin, you find delicious, nutritious fruit. But watch out for the seed in the middle. And while messy eating is not permissible in some circles, standing alone in the middle of a peach orchard allows you to relish the moment by putting aside all etiquette. So just let the juice run. When it drips from your chin onto your hands, savor the moment and lick your fingers.

So why are peaches my favorite? To me, they represent answered prayer.

I have often put my prayer seeds in the soil of faith, watching, hoping, persevering and waiting for a glimpse of developing fruit to appear. When the flowers begin to bud on the tree branches, hope for a fruitful harvest begins to develop in the heart. Jesus told us the same:

> *He told them another parable: "The kingdom of heaven is like a mustard seed, which a man took and planted in his field. Though it is the smallest of all seeds, yet when it grows, it is the largest of garden plants and becomes a tree, so that the birds come and perch in its branches."*

> Matthew 13:31-32

God likes seeds! Even as the farmer plants seeds in the soil, so the Lord plants His holy seed in us. We have been fashioned from the soil of the earth. We are the field He has chosen. As we open our hearts to the Gardener, He plants the holy seed of His Son within us. He waters it with the Word, removes the rocky calluses from our hearts, and plows through our resistance to bring forth the fruit of His Son within us. He tenderly watches over His Word, uprooting invading weeds and demonic insects that would spoil the fruit. Finally, He looks for a harvest from what has been planted. Psalm 92:12-15 says:

> *The righteous will flourish like a palm tree, they will grow like a cedar of Lebanon; planted in the house of the LORD, they will flourish in the courts of our God. They will still bear fruit in old age, they will stay fresh and green, proclaiming, "The LORD is upright; he is my Rock, and there is no wickedness in him."*

There is nothing we can do in ourselves to bring forth fruit. The fruit comes from the seed of the Son who has been allowed to grow within us. Our part is to yield to the Master Gardener. His part is to cultivate our hearts for His purposes. Sometimes this requires a little fertilizer, and sometimes this can be unpleasant. Anyone who's driven through the farm roads of Missouri in spring knows the stiff smell of raw fertilizer freshly spread on farmer's fields. Jesus talked about fertilizer when He was examining the fig tree.

> *Then he told this parable: "A man had a fig tree growing in his vineyard, and he went to look for fruit on it but did not find any. So he said to the man who took care of the vineyard, 'For three years now*

*I've been coming to look for fruit on this fig tree and haven't found any. Cut it down! Why should it use up the soil?' "'Sir,' the man replied, 'leave it alone for one more year, and I'll dig around it and fertilize it. If it bears fruit next year, fine! If not, then cut it down.'"*

Luke 13:6-9

Fertilizer is essential to bringing forth a bountiful harvest. So instead of fighting the stinky circumstances that come our way, accept them as life's fertilizer intended to bring forth a harvest of righteousness within us. Let the fruits of the holy seed come forth as described in Galatians:

*But the fruit of the Spirit is love, joy, peace, forbearance, kindness, goodness, faithfulness, gentleness and self-control. Against such things there is no law.*

Galatians 5:22-23

I love to walk through the orchard of answered prayer. Taste and see the Lord is good.

# VIII

# COMMUNICATION

*Lord,*

*I know that prayer is communication with you. I choose to walk, talk, and gain wisdom from our prayer relationship. Forgive me for reacting to others out of my soul's offense or misunderstanding. Give me utterance to say what needs to be said and refrain from saying too much. I know your Word says that the tongue is a small rudder, able to turn great ships. Put a guard over my tongue so I bless and curse not. You have given me tools to use in relationships, one of which is communication. I choose to allow my heart to be seen by others; I choose to make myself vulnerable in order to reach them with your grace and restoration. May I communicate clearly without fear. Help me dive into deeper waters when it comes to relating to others. Remove the fear of other's responses to my heart's attempt at communicating. Open my mouth that I may declare wondrous things from my relationship with you through Your Word. May the Words of my mouth and the meditations of my heart be pleasing to You my God. I choose to use the wisdom of forgiveness toward anyone who has hurt me. I ask for your grace to communicate adequately. Amen*

# Words

*And the Lord answered me and said, Write the vision and engrave it so plainly upon tablets that everyone who passes may [be able to] read [it easily and quickly] as he hastens by.*

Habakkuk 2:2 (AMP)

I am rarely at a loss for words. But not everybody has my gift of articulation. Some even desire to remain quiet. A leader of few words can seem wise, even efficient, but such reticence can actually stifle working relationships and hinder forward progress. How can a team get to the destination if they haven't been told what the destination is?

Words express thoughts and ideas. They are an integral part of communication, complementing (or contradicting) gestures, facial expressions, and body language. Words are powerful in themselves but become more so when they are conveyed to eager listeners. Words carry influence and have the power to impact culture.

Certainly, *how* we speak is crucial to being heard, but so is *when* we speak. The timing of communication drives the intended result. Here's a good example of dialog that came too late: *I wish you hadn't done that!*

This statement, while true, does little to help the situation. Instead, it speaks to something already done and implies that it can't be undone. The unintended consequence of this ill-timed utterance is to trap the recipient in the poor decision that provoked the speaker. Even though the displeasure was promptly expressed, it came too late to be productive.

So how do we escape the trap and bring true communication to the table? In this situation, there is no table of communication; communication has been tabled. Better to have discussed the situation prior to the event. But in saying this, even I am giving instruction after the fact.

I was raised in a family where very little instruction was given. We were told *what* to do but not *how* to do it. So we jumped in and tried to figure it out. Unfortunately, when things went wrong, we were corrected for not doing it properly.

So where does the fault lie? In the performance or the lack of instruction?

Given my childhood experience, I'd say it often lies in the lack of instruction. Of course, if proper instruction is given and the performer still falls short, then it lies with the performer. The culpability of either instructor or performer is one that I face frequently in my adult life, especially in my own leadership.

As a director of two non-profit organizations, I cannot expect those I work with to perform tasks correctly unless I properly instruct them. Further, I cannot expect them to see the process of preparation without first being shown that process.

Harry S. Truman famously described the responsibility of leadership when he said, "The buck stops here." A true leader will communicate vision, purpose and process to his or her team *before* performance rather than critique afterward. Complete and timely instruction avoids the *blame and shame game*, resulting in stronger teamwork that accomplishes the targeted purpose.

Conversation that conveys personal accountability is rare these days. Instead, fault-finding is in vogue. Yet, blaming others is the coward's way out. True communication expresses words that reach the heart of a matter without destroying the heart. True leadership influences, instructs, corrects, motivates, and appreciates others. A key element of this is ongoing, purposeful communication that speaks and listens.

How can a team get to the destination? Through leadership that effectively communicates.

Write it; speak it; impart it; accomplish it!

# The Red Herring

Recently I had to confront a subordinate about an error. I know to pick my battles wisely to not appear a nit-picky person and cause my people to hide from me. But for the record, the confrontation was necessary.

I picked an opportune time and made sure he knew exactly what was unacceptable about his behavior while in my employ. Indeed, I thought our conversation was going quite well until the red herring showed up. I'm sure you know what that is, but for those who need a refresher, here goes.

A red herring was used in a fox hunt to throw the hounds off the scent. It's a fish with a strong odor that overpowers the fox scent. It's a great ploy, really, to take attention from one situation and redirect to another. It's also a writer's tool used in murder mysteries to divert attention from the villain to the innocent butler.

In confrontation, it refers to refusing to take responsibility for our own actions by diverting attention and possible blame to someone or something else. When we want to avoid responsibility for our actions, we point the finger elsewhere, usually indicating that it was their fault we failed or made a poor decision.

Hmmmm! Let's face it. It works pretty well unless the smell of the red herring is so overpowering, it is recognized and thrown out of the conversation. Things also get interesting when both people throw out a few red herrings. The scent of the red herrings causes the hounds to run in circles, never reaching the fox. Point taken!

Ever wondered why communication is difficult these days? Just maybe, the blame/shame game overpowers the goal of real conversation. Owning our mistakes and even apologizing for them is actually the mature response to being caught in an error. Real communication eschews defensive tactics and strikes for the heart of a matter. Why can't we just talk to each other, own our mistakes, apologize, and move on?

Part of the problem is that we somehow associate our mistakes with our identity. We confuse making an error with being an error. Let's be clear. We are not a mistake when we make a mistake. What we do is not who we are. *Who we are* is internal and pertains to the heart. *What we do* is external and can be changed through a change of heart.

So let's eat red herring as a delicacy and keep it out of our conversations. The point of the fox hunt is to catch the fox! And the goal of conversation is to reach the heart. Face to face, eye to eye, heart to heart communication is rare these days, but so vital for healthy relationships.

# Optional Listening

I admire opera singers. They sing from a deep place. Not only does it come from their diaphragm, but from their heart as well. Their voices can envelop a stage and fill a concert hall, delivering a sound that impacts anybody listening.

At the opera, you pay to take in what they are selling. Therefore, to get your money's worth, you would likely tune your senses to the performance. In this setting, you-the-listener are paying to hear a performance.

But sometimes it's the other way around. People are so desperate to be heard that they pay someone to listen to them. It's called counseling or mentoring or buying lunch for a friend.

So why are people willing to pay money to be heard? Because they want someone to really listen to them, and good listeners are rare.

Are you a good listener? If I were to answer for myself, I'd say sometimes I am and sometimes I'm not. There are times when I am not thinking about what is being said but instead, anxiously waiting for a pause so I can jump in with my comments. (I'm sure I'm not alone in this.)

Listening is a purposeful posture that has lost much of its value in today's culture. Perhaps it's because there is so much for our senses to process that we tend to tune out what we deem unnecessary. Listening goes beyond processing words; it's bigger than that. Behind the spoken word is a heart that is trying to express what it feels, sees, and knows. Discounting distracted hearing, are we really listening to what is being said?

Want to take the challenge? Here it is. Make a point to really listen to someone this week. It will be an eye-opener. (Even an ear-opener!) You will have to keep your mind from being distracted; you will have to intentionally focus on what is being said, and hear with the ears of wisdom to capture the silent sounds of another heart.

> *My son, if you accept my words and store up my commands within you, turning your ear to wisdom and applying your heart to understanding—indeed, if you call out for insight and cry aloud for understanding, and if you look for it as for silver and search for it as for hidden treasure, then you will understand the fear of the Lord and find the knowledge of God.*
>
> Proverbs 2:1-5

# Bouncing Words

Words came bouncing out like ink from a pen. They were everywhere. The key was to select the right words and put them in the right order. To do this, I had to pick the language. For most of us, there is little choice but to choose our mother tongue. Of course, there are over 6500 languages in the world. For your benefit and mine, I chose English. It's for your benefit, so you can read this. It's for my benefit so I can write it. Now we have narrowed our word options considerably. But they are still bouncing, waiting to be chosen.

Words are quite canny. They have broad definitions, so when choosing them, you must know what they mean. There are nouns and verbs. Some verbs bounce around like children on a trampoline. Some link your sentence together so it won't lie on the paper like a cut sandwich. There are also adjectives, prepositions, adverbs, conjunctions and so on. You might ask, *"Is there a point here?"* Of course there is—that's called punctuation.

I have this pet peeve. I want the verb to agree with the noun. (I've had a few very good English teachers along the way who agree.) So when someone says, "I done this," or "I done that," I want to correct them so badly my teeth crunch and my tongue needs stitches. I've even had to ask friends to watch over me and be my mouth guard.

With all these bouncing words, do we ever say something we shouldn't? It's so hard to get those words back after they have been spoken. They roll out of the mouth and bounce in every direction. It gets worse if someone picks them up and repeats them to others, especially when they add their own twist to the original words. You can't get them back. Once released, there is no retrieval. Cleaning up that kind of mess is like mopping up mud from barn boots.

I remember the story, *A Pillow Full of Feathers*, by Shoshannah Brombacher. It's about a man who gossiped about others. His words were like a pillow of feathers released in the wind. It was impossible to retrieve them all. I never forgot that lesson.

Words can hurt or heal. Words can comfort or steal. Words communicate the heart. Words bounce from pen and fly with the wind. Choose them well!

> *A good man brings good things out of the good stored up in his heart, and an evil man brings evil things out of the evil stored up in his heart. For the mouth speaks what the heart is full of.*

> Luke 6:45

# Canopy Of Green

The GPS was taking me along an unexpected route of narrow country roads winding through hills and over creeks. Tree branches stretched across the road, creating a canopy of green. The sun glittered through the leaves in emerald light. I had a destination in mind, but the rolling hills, verdant pastures, and quaint farmhouses were refreshing my soul. I couldn't bear to listen to music—my usual companion when traveling alone. The quiet serenity and natural beauty drew me into a peaceful abode.

My soul was at rest, a part of the scene. Everything has its place, its purpose, its natural beauty, and I was finding mine passing through new territory I would probably never see again. I had to savor this moment—remember and cherish it. I sought to capture it, but instead it captured me.

Wildflowers waved from the roadside. Yellow butterflies fluttered across my windshield. White trumpet blossoms blew silent blasts heralding my arrival. It was a wakeup call from God Himself. "Trust me," He seemed to say. "I created all this and planned this moment just for us. Your road is turning just like this one. I'm taking you to places you have never been to see beauty you've never seen. You will travel through hills and valleys, cross over wooden bridges I built to carry you over creeks you could never navigate by yourself. I am opening your eyes to see with greater clarity. Do not lose this gift of peace and serenity I am giving you today. It is a substance

I want to deposit inside your soul that will grow as you grasp the reality of who I Am inside you. I Am giving you rest. Be still and know that I am God!"

The mechanical voice of my GPS directed me to my next turn. As I entered the interstate, I knew I had already reached my destination despite the miles I had left to travel. An encounter with the Creator and Lover of my soul had changed me forever. Perhaps my GPS had been rerouted by the One who knew a narrow road through the countryside could strengthen me for the road ahead.

# IX

# PRAYER

## *Crying Out for America*

Forgive us Father for choosing our own way, for allowing our fleshly desires to rule instead of listening to your loving, protective voice directing us to the path of life. We have strayed from your ways, believing you would understand and allow us to go our own way without consequences. We have occasionally thrown a prayer your way, expecting you to hear our casual petitions for grace. Yet we rarely take time to seek your face, know your heart, or desire to walk in your ways.

We have lowered you to our standards and expected you to accept our ignoble ways and practices. We have stolen your church and made it ours, allowing secular ways and cultural norms to penetrate and destroy true worship and righteous living. Our focus has been ourselves. Our casual approach to Biblical values has lowered our expectations of ourselves and others to mere human standards.

We have taken prayer out of schools, killed our unborn, sold their parts, destroyed the structure of marriage, and assumed you would understand our choice to live ungodly lifestyles. We have allowed our minds to be filled with the garbage of unprincipled creations of man in entertainment, allowed the deception of tolerance for all. This has tainted our judgment and compromised our standards. We have fallen so short of your glory that we don't even realize the depth to which we have descended.

Father, please touch our stony hearts and cause us to feel again; cause us to care about what you want; cause us to wake from the matrix of unprincipled living and depart from delusional, unteachable, rebellious ways. Forgive us for tolerating everything and everyone whose dissenting voice reaches our ears for fear we will be accused of being judgmental or critical. Forgive us for blaming you for the mess we have created, for being silent when we could have spoken out against ungodliness, fearing we might offend. Have we fallen so far that the approval of man has become our ecstasy and fleshly pursuits our goal? Have we allowed Truth to fall in the streets and not bent our knee to pick it up again?

Hear our cry, oh Lord. Do not leave America in this fallen state! Visit us with a move of your Spirit that will awaken us, cause us to cry out in repentance, hear from Heaven, and heal our land.

Amen

# Biography

Regina Shank has written numerous articles, poems, and devotions published in a variety of publications. Her column, Blessed in Carthage, is published by *The Carthage Press*, in Carthage, MO. She is the founder and President of Missouri Prayer Global Ministries (an apostolic ministry aligned with Network Ekklesia International with Apostle Dutch Sheets, and Global Spheres with Chuck Pierce.) She also is the founder and director of Feeding Inc a feeding outreach ministry in southwest Missouri. Regina teaches on prayer, prophetic and strategic intercession, warfare, and the importance of a strong personal relationship with Jesus. She has served in several leadership roles in the body of Christ, leading prayer trips to Romania, Italy, Bosnia, Ethiopia, Egypt, Israel, Hungary, Russia, and China. She and her husband, Mick, have three children and five grandchildren. Mick is a real estate appraiser and the mayor of their small community in southwest Missouri.

Made in the USA
Monee, IL
01 May 2025

16722515R00085